C.T. STUDD
CRICKETER AND MISSIONARY

ILLUSTRATED IN FULL COLOUR

C.T. STUDD

CRICKETER and MISSIONARY
ILLUSTRATED

Drawn by

EDMUND JULIAN

A *wec* PUBLICATION

ISBN 0 900828 41 2

WEC PUBLICATIONS,
Bulstrode, Oxford Road,
Gerrards Cross, Bucks, SL9 8SZ

Drawings by Edmund Julian
Text by Christopher Scott
Colouring by Alison Hunt and John Tromans
Cover by Eddie Julian

PRINTED OFFSET LITHO IN GREAT BRITAIN
BY WEC PRESS, GERRARDS CROSS, BUCKS.

SOME stories fade, then die. But not this one. The adventure is as alive now as when it first began, for C.T. Studd was no ordinary cricketer and no ordinary missionary. His fame on the field of sport was outstripped by that on the field of missionary service.

The tangible outcome of his dedication and sacrifice is the mission known as WEC. He was the founder of a team of ready-for-anything followers of Christ; a team, now numbering over 1,000, active in over 40 countries of the world, through whom the adventure continues.

Edmund Julian, the artist, through reading the biography of C.T. Studd, found himself compelled to capture some of the details of this adventurous life. His active imagination and skill as a successful illustrator were balanced by an awareness of the importance of accuracy. Thorough research has resulted in a document of simplest form, yet with historical, cultural and physical details correct.

Julian discovered, for example, that the school uniform at Eton was peculiarly different when C.T. Studd was there as a boy. The locomotive standing in the station pictured in the farewell scene perfectly dates the incident. The same care was taken in the composition of the illustrations: each picture mattered. He was satisfied only when the result was worthy of the purpose for which they had been drawn — to make alive the simple dedication, utter sacrifice and unfaltering faith of a man and his wife, for Mrs Studd majors in the story too.

The story begins with the conversion of C.T. Studd's father who had been a wealthy tea planter in India. The vigorous preaching of D.L. Moody won him to Christ. Thrilled by his great discovery, he sought to win his sons, servants and neighbours for Christ. Preachers were invited to his beautiful mansion home in Wiltshire for weekends, where drawing-room gatherings were arranged. The illustrations take up the story at this point.

CHARLTON SMITH

C.T. STUDD
CRICKETER and MISSIONARY

C.T'S FATHER HELD MEETINGS IN HIS HOME TO TELL PEOPLE ABOUT JESUS.

ON ONE OCCASION C.T. AND HIS BROTHERS THOUGHT A PARTICULAR SPEAKER, RATHER DULL.

WE'LL PLAY A JOKE ON MR WHETHERBY. HE'S A SOFTIE.

THE BROTHERS LATER INVITED THE SPEAKER TO GO RIDING

IF WE GALLOP PAST .... SUDDENLY HE WON'T BE ABLE TO HOLD HIS HORSE.

EDMUND JULIAN

7

THEIR PLAN WAS SUCCESSFUL

THEY REPEATED THIS TRICK SEVERAL TIMES

THEIR FATHER COULD NOT REBUKE THEM BECAUSE OF HIS OWN LAUGHTER

YOU ARE A GOOD FELLOW, WHETHERBY, TAKING IT ALL SO WELL.

WAS'NT THAT FUN BAITING WHETHERBY!

THAT AFTERNOON · · · ·

CHARLIE, ARE YOU A CHRISTIAN?

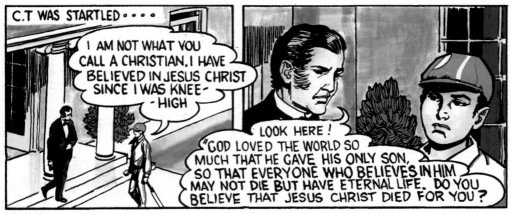

9

THERE WAS NOTHING ELSE TO DO BUT TO GET DOWN ON MY KNEES AND THANK GOD RIGHT THERE. JOY AND PEACE CAME INTO MY HEART. I KNEW I WAS BORN AGAIN. THE BIBLE WHICH WAS SO DRY BEFORE BECAME EVERYTHING TO ME

AND SO BACK TO SCHOOL

THEN C.T. WROTE TO HIS FATHER BUT SAID NOTHING TO HIS BROTHERS, GEORGE AND KYNASTON

FATHER WILL BE SURPRISED

FROM THE BOYS

OUR BOYS HAVE EACH ACCEPTED THE LORD JESUS AS THEIR SAVIOUR ON THE SAME DAY, UNKNOWN TO EACH OTHER.

WHILST C.T. STUDD AND HIS BROTHERS WERE AT ETON THEY STARTED A BIBLE CLASS

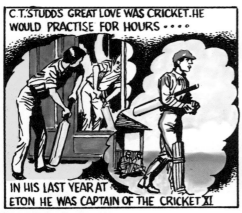

C.T. STUDD'S GREAT LOVE WAS CRICKET. HE WOULD PRACTISE FOR HOURS....

IN HIS LAST YEAR AT ETON HE WAS CAPTAIN OF THE CRICKET XI

FROM ETON HE WENT UP TO TRINITY COLLEGE CAMBRIDGE WHERE CRICKET WAS STILL HIS GREATEST INTEREST. HE PLAYED WITH TREMENDOUS SUCCESS FOR CAMBRIDGE AGAINST THE AUSTRALIANS, LANCASHIRE, THE CHAMPION COUNTY AND OXFORD, WHEN THEY WON EVERY MATCH

EVANGELIST
MOODY MISSION

FOR SIX YEARS HE DID NOT BOTHER ABOUT GOD, UNTIL THE SERIOUS ILLNESS OF HIS BROTHER GEORGE MADE HIM THINK AGAIN.

WHAT IS POPULARITY OR FAME WORTH TO GEORGE NOW, OR ALL THE RICHES IN THE WORLD, WHEN FACE TO FACE WITH DEATH?

C.T. SPENT THREE MONTHS READING HIS BIBLE AND PRAYING FOR GUIDANCE.

CHINA

HE DECIDED TO GO TO CHINA AS A MISSIONARY

OPPOSITION

CHARLIE, I THINK YOU ARE MAKING A MISTAKE. YOU ARE AWAY EVERY NIGHT AT THE MEETINGS AND YOU DO NOT SEE YOUR MOTHER. IT IS JUST BREAKING HER HEART TO THINK OF YOU GOING SO FAR AWAY AS CHINA.

AN ANSWER

"A MAN'S FOES SHALL BE OF HIS OWN HOUSEHOLD."

I KNOW THAT IT IS GOD'S VOICE SPEAKING TO ME AND I HAVE RECEIVED MY MARCHING ORDERS TO GO TO CHINA

THE FAREWELL MEETING

C.T. HAD AN INTERVIEW WITH HUDSON TAYLOR OF THE CHINA INLAND MISSION. HE WAS ACCEPTED AS AN ASSOCIATE MEMBER. SOON, AFTER MANY MEETINGS TELLING OF THE CALL TO CHINA, C.T., WITH SIX OTHER YOUNG MEN, SAILED FOR CHINA IN FEBRUARY, 1885.

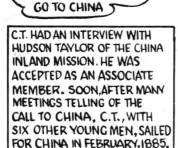

DURING THE VOYAGE THE SEVEN WITNESSED TO CHRIST

I DON'T BELIEVE THAT ROT! BAH! RELIGION!

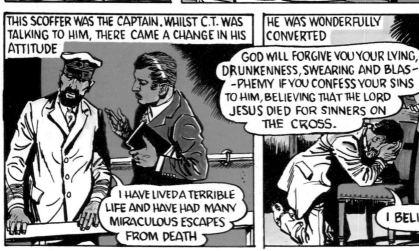

THIS SCOFFER WAS THE CAPTAIN. WHILST C.T. WAS TALKING TO HIM, THERE CAME A CHANGE IN HIS ATTITUDE

I HAVE LIVED A TERRIBLE LIFE AND HAVE HAD MANY MIRACULOUS ESCAPES FROM DEATH

HE WAS WONDERFULLY CONVERTED

GOD WILL FORGIVE YOU YOUR LYING, DRUNKENNESS, SWEARING AND BLAS--PHEMY IF YOU CONFESS YOUR SINS TO HIM, BELIEVING THAT THE LORD JESUS DIED FOR SINNERS ON THE CROSS.

I BELIEVE

THREE MONTHS AFTER THEIR ARRIVAL IN CHINA

HOW DO I LOOK?

HAVE I MET YOU BEFORE?

C.T.'S LARGE FEET CAUSED MERR-IMENT TO THE CHINESE

THE CAMBRIDGE SEVEN SEPARATED AND WENT TO VARIOUS PARTS OF CHINA, C.T. GOING NORTHWARDS TO PINGYANG AND TAI-YUEN.

TIME WAS SPENT IN LEARNING THE LANGUAGE.

I WISH THAT YOU COULD SPEAK JUST A FEW WORDS OF ENGLISH

LATER HE SET OUT FOR HANCHUNG WITH TWO OTHERS OF THE CAMBRIDGE SEVEN. THE POLHILL-TURNER BROTHERS.

THIS JOURNEY TOOK THEM THREE MONTHS

RATS!

THE RATS WERE SUCH A PROB-LEM THAT THEY ASKED GOD TO GET RID OF THEM. FROM THEN ON THEY HAD NO MORE TROUBLE.

FROM HANCHUNG HE WENT TO PINGYANG TO MEET HUDSON TAYLOR. ON THE JOURNEY HE SUFFERED GREATLY FROM SORE FEET.

HIS FEET BECAME PUFFY AND SEPTIC.

WILL YOU ANOINT ME WITH OIL IN THE NAME OF THE LORD AS IN JAMES 5. v. 14 and 15.

THE MISSIONARY HESITATED AT FIRST, BUT AFTER THEY HAD READ FROM THE BIBLE AND PRAYED, HE WAS WILLING.

FROM THAT TIME C.T.'S FEET BEGAN TO HEAL

C.T. BEGAN HIS DAY WITH PRAYER AND BIBLE READING.
AFTER BREAK-FAST, PRAYERS WITH THE CHINESE. LATER, READING WITH THE EVANGELIST AND AFTERWARDS, THE DISTRIBUTION OF TRACTS.

HE JOURNEYED TO HANCHUNG WITH HUDSON TAYLOR

HAVE YOU HEARD? THEY ARE RIOTING IN SZCHUAN

WILL ANY GO INTO SZCHUAN?

THE SZCHUAN RIOTS!! FOREIGNERS HAD TO FLEE FROM CHUNGKING

C.T. AND ANOTHER MISSIONARY WERE CHOSEN TO RE-ENTER SZCHUAN TO PREACH GOD'S MESSAGE, BUT ON THE JOURNEY·····

NO! YOU CANNOT SLEEP HERE!

··· THE INNKEEPERS WOULD NOT TAKE THEM IN, FEARING THEIR FELLOW-COUNTRYMEN.

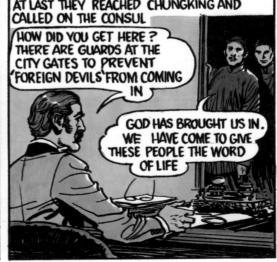

AT LAST THEY REACHED CHUNGKING AND CALLED ON THE CONSUL

HOW DID YOU GET HERE? THERE ARE GUARDS AT THE CITY GATES TO PREVENT 'FOREIGN DEVILS' FROM COMING IN

GOD HAS BROUGHT US IN. WE HAVE COME TO GIVE THESE PEOPLE THE WORD OF LIFE

15

BUT YOU CAN'T STAY HERE. IT IS IMPOSSIBLE

AFTER TALKING THINGS OVER DURING DINNER, TO WHICH THEY WERE INVITED, THE CONSUL TURNED TO C.T. STUDD

STUDD, WILL YOU STAY WITH ME?

NOW I WONDER WHY GOD HAS SENT ME TO THIS PLACE?

GOD HAD BEEN PREPAR-ING FOR THIS TIME. AT THE AGE OF 25 C.T. STUDD WAS TO INHERIT A LARGE FORTUNE. BEFORE LEAVING ENGLAND HE HAD HAD AN INTERVIEW WITH HUDSON TAYLOR CONCERNING HIS FOR-TUNE. HE WAS IMPRESS-ED BY THE WORDS OF JESUS "SELL ALL YOUR BELONGINGS AND GIVE THE MONEY TO THE POOR" AND "DO NOT LAY UP TREASURE ON EARTH"

HE REMEMBERED HIS INTERVIEW WITH HUDSON TAYLOR

I HAVE COME TO A DECISION AND WILL GIVE AWAY MY ENTIRE FORTUNE

THERE ARE TWO YEARS YET BEFORE YOU ACTUALLY INHERIT THIS FORTUNE

NOW THE TIME HAD COME ooo A SOLICITOR'S LETTER

SO MY INHERITANCE IS ABOUT £29,000. NOW I KNOW WHY I WAS SENT HERE

"HAPPY IS THE MAN WHO TRUSTS IN THE LORD" ONLY IN HEAVEN WILL WE KNOW HOW MANY HAVE BEEN ROUSED TO FACE THE REAL MEANING OF DISCIPLESHIP IN THIS TWENTIETH CENTURY "RICH YOUNG MAN" WHO DID LEAVE ALL AND FOLLOW JESUS.

IT WAS NECESSARY FOR C.T. TO GET THE SIGNATURE OF A QUEENS OFFICER BEFORE DISPOSING OF HIS FORTUNE

I WILL NOT SIGN. THINK IT OVER AND COME BACK IN A FORTNIGHT

STUDD DID RETURN AND THE CONSUL SIGNED THE DOCUMENT

ON JANUARY 13 TH. 1887 HE SENT OFF NINE CHEQUES

£5000 GEORGE MULLER
£5000 SALVATION ARMY (India)
MISS Mc.PHERSON
£5000 GEORGE HOLLAND
MISS SMYLY
REV. BROWN £1000
GEN. BOOTH
BARNADO'S HOME

C.T. STUDD MET AND FELL IN LOVE WITH A YOUNG IRISH MISSIONARY PRISCILLA STEWART.

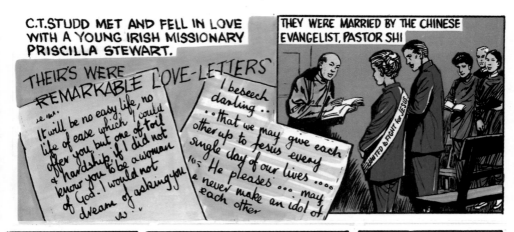

THEY WERE MARRIED BY THE CHINESE EVANGELIST, PASTOR SHI

THEIR'S WERE REMARKABLE LOVE-LETTERS

It will be no easy life, no life of ease which I could offer you, but one of toil & hardship, if I did not know you to be a woman of God. I would not dream of asking you...

I beseech darling ...that we may give each other up to Jesus every single day of our lives .... He pleases ... may we never make an idol of each other

THE YOUNG COUPLE WENT STRAIGHT FROM THEIR WEDDING CEREMONY TO WORK AT LUNGANG-FU, ACCOMPANIED BY M^{ISS} BURROUGHES, A FRIEND AND FELLOW-WORKER OF M^{RS} STUDD'S

THEIR FIRST HOME WAS A HAUNTED HOUSE

FOR FIVE YEARS THEY WERE GREETED WITH CURSES AND ABUSE

EVERYTHING THAT WENT WRONG IN THE CITY WAS BLAMED ON THEM

WE NEED RAIN

YES, THE FOREIGN DEVILS ARE TO BLAME FOR THIS DROUGHT

GRADUALLY, BY ALLOWING THE PEOPLE TO PRY INTO THEIR POSSESS--IONS THEY BECAME ON MORE FAMILIAR TERMS

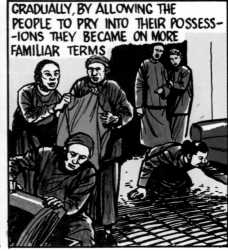

AS THE DROUGHT CONTINUED THE CHINESE BORROWED THE RAIN GOD FROM A DISTANT CITY FIVE DAYS JOURNEY AWAY

BURN INCENSE TO OUR RAIN GOD

WARNING KEEP YOUR GATES SHUT BEWARE

THEY KNOW WE WON'T BURN INCENSE, THAT MEANS THEY WILL PROBABLY ATTACK OUR HOUSE WE MUST SEND OUR CHINESE CHRISTIANS HOME.

MRS STUDD WAS ILL AT THE TIME

YOU WILL BE SAFER OUT HERE IN THE COURT-YARD

GOD TAKE CARE OF YOU! I'LL GO TO ASK HELP OF THE MANDARIN

MEANWHILE

THEY ARE DISHONOURING OUR GOD.

19

THIS MAN NOW FELT THAT HE MUST GO BACK TO HIS OWN HOME TOWN.

I MUST GO BACK TO THE TOWN WHERE I HAVE DONE SO MUCH EVIL, AND IN THAT PLACE TELL THE GOOD NEWS OF JESUS.

SO HE WENT BACK AND WITNESSED • • • •

SO HE WENT BACK • • •

JESUS SAVED ME FROM ALL MY SINS

HE WAS TAKEN BEFORE THE MANDARIN

I SENTENCE YOU TO 2000 STROKES WITH THE BAMBOO FOR DISHONOURING OUR GODS

AND SO THE SENTENCE WAS CRUELLY CARRIED OUT

LEFT FOR DEAD!

21

FRIENDS FOUND HIM AND CARRIED HIM TO A CHRISTIAN HOSPITAL

BRING HIM THIS WAY

AFTER MANY DAYS OF PAIN AND WEAKNESS HE RECOVERED

I MUST GO BACK AGAIN TO MY CITY AND PREACH THIS GOSPEL

OH! NO! THEY MAY BEAT YOU AGAIN. THEY WILL KILL YOU. WE DON'T ADVISE IT.

BUT HE GOT AWAY WITHOUT ANYONE KNOWING

BACK IN HIS CITY HE AGAIN TOLD EVERY--ONE THAT JESUS COULD FORGIVE THEIR SINS AND CHANGE THEIR LIVES.

THE MANDARIN WAS ASHAMED TO PUNISH HIM WITH THE BAMBOO AGAIN, SO PUT HIM IN PRISON••

•• WHERE HE PREACHED TO SMALL CROWDS OUTSIDE

FINDING HIS PREACHING FROM PRISON MORE EFFECTIVE THAN WHEN FREE, THE AUTHORITIES DESPAIRED OF EVER STOPPING HIM, SO LET HIM GO FREE.

ANOTHER MISSION OF THE STUDDS WAS TO THE OPIUM VICTIMS

OPIUM REFUGE

BUT WE MUST HELP YOU

OPIUM RE

IN 7 YEARS 800 MEN AND WOMEN PASSED THROUGH THE REFUGE. MANY WERE SAVED AS WELL AS CURED

FOUR LITTLE GIRLS WERE BORN TO THE STUDDS TO BRIGHTEN THEIR CHINESE HOME

NOW GIRLS WERE NOT WANTED BY CHINESE PARENTS

WHAT IS THE MATTER?

MY BABY WAS A GIRL ••• THEY HAVE TAKEN HER TO THE PAGODA

THESE PAGODAS WERE BUILT FOR THIS PURPOSE

ONE OF THE CURSES OF CHINA AT THIS PERIOD WAS THE CUSTOM OF NOT LETTING THEIR LITTLE GIRLS LIVE. THEY SAID THAT THE MARRIAGE DOWRY DID NOT MAKE UP FOR ALL THAT HAD BEEN SPENT ON THEM

GOD GAVE ME FOUR LITTLE GIRLS. HE GAVE THEM FOR A PURPOSE. HE WANTED THESE PEOPLE TO LEARN THAT GOD LOVES LITTLE GIRLS AS WELL AS LITTLE BOYS

THERE WAS ALSO THE MATERIAL SIDE OF LIFE AND MIRACLES OF GOD'S PROVIDING

THE LAST OF OUR SUPPLIES IS FINISHED. IF NO HELP COMES BY THE NEXT MAIL WE SHALL STARVE.

WE MUST TELL THE LORD ALL OUR NEEDS

TOGETHER THEY HAD A TIME OF PRAYER

THE LORD KNOWS BEFORE WE ASK HIM··· "BEFORE THEY CALL I WILL ANSWER"··· WE MUST JUST WAIT ON HIM

THE POSTMAN CAME····· THEY OPENED ALL THE LETTERS

THERE IS NOTHING

ARE YOU SURE THERE IS NOTHING IN THE SACK?

A LETTER FROM AN UNKNOWN HAND

WHAT DOES IT SAY?

or other for some reason of God to send you a cheque for £100. I have never met you, I have only heard of you and that not often, but God has prevented me from sleeping tonight by this command. Why He should command me to send you this I don't know···· you know better than I. Anyway here it is and I hope that it will do you good.

AND SO GOODBYE TO CHINA···

GOOD-BYE

··AND RETURN TO ENGLAND

WELL, MR. STUDD YOU DIDN'T COME TO CHINA FOR NOTHING

24

THEY ARRIVED HOME IN LONDON EVENTUALLY AND WERE WARMLY WELCOMED BY C.T's MOTHER.

C.T. GOT WELL AGAIN BUT MRS. STUDD WAS STILL UNWELL. THEY WOULD NOT BE ABLE TO RETURN TO CHINA

I AM INVITED TO AMERICA FOR EIGHTEEN MONTHS TO CONDUCT STUDENT MEETINGS

SOMETIMES HE HAD AS MANY AS SIX MEETINGS A DAY. HE SELDOM SPOKE FOR LESS THAN AN HOUR

BUT MOST OF THE WORK WAS DONE IN PRIVATE INTERVIEWS

AS CHRIST DIED FOR YOU, YOU BELONG BY RIGHTS TO HIM

WILL YOU YIELD YOURSELF AND ALL YOU HAVE TO JESUS?

YES, LORD JESUS. I GIVE MYSELF TO THEE. SAVE ME NOW. AMEN.

NOW ASK GOD FOR THE HOLY SPIRIT TO FILL YOUR WHOLE LIFE. THEN THANK HIM FOR DOING IT

HAVE YOU BEEN FORGIVEN AND RECEIVED THE HOLY SPIRIT?

YES. GLORY TO GOD

ALWAYS TRUST HIM AND OBEY HIS VOICE

IN 1900 C.T. AND HIS FAMILY SAILED FOR INDIA.

HE PREACHED TO THE PLANTERS AT TIRHOOT

HE HELD MEETINGS IN A NEIGHBOURING SOLDIERS HOME

C.T. HAD ALWAYS WANTED TO PREACH THERE WHERE HIS FATHER MADE HIS WEALTH. THEY STAYED FOR SIX YEARS.

PASTORED A CHURCH AT OOTACAMUND

C.T. TOOK UP CRICKET AGAIN AND HIS OLD FORM RETURNED. IN 1904 HE MADE TWO DOUBLE CENTURIES WHICH HAD ONLY BEEN DONE ONCE PREVIOUSLY IN INDIAN CRICKET.

THE REAL REASON WAS SO THAT HE COULD HOLD MEETINGS FOR SOLDIERS AFTER THEY HAD PLAYED THE REGIMENTAL TEAMS

HIS OWN GIRLS WERE CONVERTED AND BAPTIZED

THE FAMILY RETURNED TO
ENGLAND IN 1906.
C.T. STUDD TOOK MEETINGS
ALL OVER THE COUNTRY,
SPEAKING TO MEN ABOUT
JESUS CHRIST.
THEN ONE DAY ....

LIVERPOOL 1908

CANNIBALS WANT MISSIONARIES

SURE THEY DO! FOR MORE REASONS THAN ONE!

IN THE HEART OF AFRICA, HUNTERS AND TRADERS HAVE GONE, BUT NO ONE TO TELL OF JESUS

I MUST GO THERE!

WE WILL CROSS AFRICA FROM THE NIGER SIDE

BUT C.T. WENT DOWN WITH AN ATTACK OF MALARIA AND COULD NOT GO.

SOME BUSINESSMEN FORMED THEMSELVES INTO A COMMITTEE

WE WILL PAY YOUR EXPENSES IF THE DOCTOR PASSES YOU AS FIT.

I CANNOT PASS YOU! YOU WILL DIE IF YOU GO TO THE TROPICS

28

HOW COULD ONE MAN'S JOURNEY TO A CORNER OF THE SUDAN DO SOMETHING FOR ALL TRIBES AND PEOPLE WHO HAVE NEVER HEARD OF JESUS? IT SEEMED IMPOSSIBLE, BUT C.T. STUDD BELIEVED GOD.

HE WROTE TO A FRIEND

I SEEM TO HEAR JESUS SAYING 'GO OVER AND POSSESS THE GOOD LAND OF THE WORLD'

TO HIS WIFE HE WROTE

I think and think and think and all on the same line — a new crusade. It burns in my brain and heart. It must be!

FROM KHARTOUM HE MADE A TWO AND A HALF MONTHS TREK OF EXPLORATION WITH A BISHOP AND C.M.S MISSIONARY

THE PEOPLE ARE NEEDY BUT FEW. WE CANNOT START A NEW MISSION HERE

WE WILL EXTEND OUR WORK TO COVER THIS AREA

SOUTH OF OUR COUNTRY, OVER THE BORDER, THERE ARE MANY PEOPLE

MILLIONS TO BE REACHED FOR CHRIST IN THE CONGO THAT IS WHERE WE MUST START IT

C.T. SAILED DOWN THE NILE AND RETURNED TO BRITAIN TO LAUNCH THE NEW CRUSADE

HE WROTE BOOKLETS TO STIR UP PEOPLE FOR CHRIST

HE ADDRESSED MEETINGS UP AND DOWN THE COUNTRY

ONE YOUNG CAMBRIDGE STUDENT VOLUNTEERED TO GO WITH HIM

IS IT A FACT THAT AT 52 YOU MEAN TO LEAVE YOUR COUNTRY, YOUR HOME, YOUR WIFE AND YOUR CHILDREN?

WE HAVE TALKED OF SACRIFICE TONIGHT! IF JESUS CHRIST BE GOD AND DIED FOR ME, THEN NO SACRIFICE CAN BE TOO GREAT FOR ME TO MAKE FOR HIM.

THIS LAST SENTENCE BECAME THE MOTTO OF THE NEW CRUSADE

C.T. STUDD
AND
YOUNG ALFRED BUXTON
SAILED FOR AFRICA,
ACCOMPANIED BY THREE
OTHERS FOR THE FIRST PART
OF THE JOURNEY. THERE
WERE MANY PROBLEMS.

THEY LANDED AT MOMBASSA AND JOURNEYED THROUGH KENYA AND UGANDA TO LAKE ALBERT

THE BELGIANS WON'T LET YOU IN BECAUSE YOU'RE BRITISH

THAT REMAINS TO BE SEEN. I GO TO PROVE IT.

IT IS SUCH A DANGEROUS JOURNEY I DON'T SEE HOW YOU CAN SURVIVE IT.

THEY MET WITH MANY DIFFICULTIES

ALFRED WENT DOWN WITH FEVER

THEIR CAMP CAUGHT FIRE

THAT'S OUT, BUT WE HAVE LOST ONE OF OUR TENTS AS WELL AS OTHER EQUIPMENT

A CABLE FOR YOU ALFRED

FROM MY RELATIVES. THEY SAY I'M NOT SUITABLE AND SHOULD GO BACK.

WELL?

GOD HAS CALLED ME. I MUST GO ON!

THEY CROSSED LAKE ALBERT AND ENTERED CONGO

THAT IS QUITE ALL RIGHT MR STUDD. YOU MAY PROCEED

WHERE ARE THE PORTERS? WE HAVE LOST THEM!

THEY FOUND THEIR EQUIPMENT AGAIN, AND REACHED KILO, A GOLD MINING CENTRE

C.T. WAS TAKEN ILL WITH FEVER SEVERAL TIMES

I AM VERY ILL. I FEAR THE WORST. TOMORROW YOU MAY BE ALONE

WHAT WILL YOU DO?

I SHALL GO ON

GOOD MAN!

WAIT! WHAT DOES THE SCRIPTURE SAY IN JAMES 5 v.14.?

IS ANY SICK AMONG YOU? LET HIM CALL FOR THE ELDERS OF THE CHURCH, AND LET THEM PRAY OVER HIM, ANOINTING HIM WITH OIL IN THE NAME OF THE LORD; AND THE PRAYER OF FAITH SHALL SAVE THE SICK, AND THE LORD SHALL RAISE HIM UP.
James 5 v. 14-15

THE ONLY OIL WE HAVE IS LAMP OIL

AND YOU ARE THE ONLY ELDER — AGED 20! USE IT! WE HAVE NO OTHER

ALFRED ANOINTED HIM WITH OIL AND PRAYED

34

NEXT MORNING

YOU ARE WELL AGAIN! GOD HAS HEALED YOU!

WE TRUST GOD TOO LITTLE, BUT WE CANNOT TRUST HIM TOO MUCH

THEY TREKKED FOR ELEVEN DAYS THROUGH THE GREAT ITURI FOREST

AT LAST THEY REACHED NIANGARA IN THE VERY HEART OF AFRICA

THE JOURNEY HAD TAKEN THEM NINE MONTHS

THIS WILL BE A GOOD SPOT TO BUILD OUR MISSION STATION

NEXT DAY

YOU CANNOT HAVE THIS LAND!

WHAT SHALL WE DO?

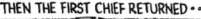

THEN THE FIRST CHIEF RETURNED...

THEY BUILT THEIR FIRST MISSION HOUSE FOR SIX POUNDS

BWANA, COME! THERE'S A SNAKE IN YOUR BED!

IT'S BITE IS DEATH!

YOU SLEPT WITH IT ALL LAST NIGHT!

GOD HAS KEPT HIS PROMISE IN PSALM 91: v.11 "GOD WILL PUT HIS ANGELS IN CHARGE OF YOU TO PROTECT YOU" HE IS ALWAYS FAITHFUL

THE GOVERNMENT ASKED C.T. STUDD TO GO DOWN TO NALA TO SETTLE THE BOUNDARIES OF THE NEW CON- -CESSION. THIS SEEMED GOD'S CALL TO A MORE EXTENDED TRIP TO THE SOUTH, RIGHT INTO THE ITURI PRO- -VINCE WHICH THEY HEARD TEEMED WITH PEOPLE. IT WAS AT A TIME WHEN C.T WAS BEING PRESSED TO RETURN HOME TO ENGLAND. BUT GOD IMPRESSED ON HIM THAT HE MUST SEE THAT COUNTRY FIRST

THEY MADE A SURVEY SOUTH OF NALA, AND FOUND THOUSANDS OF PEOPLE WHO WELCOMED THEM GLADLY

THEY MADE ONE LONG TREK AND CHOSE TWO OTHER CENTRES FOR WORK AT POKO AND BAMBILI, THEN • • • • •

BACK HOME HE WROTE STIRRING ARTICLES FOR THE MISSIONARY MAGAZINE

FIVE MORE RECRUITS ARE ON THEIR WAY TO JOIN US

YOU MUST REMAIN HERE TO ESTABLISH THE WORK. I WILL RETURN TO ENGLAND FOR MORE RECRUITS.

HE ADDRESSED MEETINGS UP AND DOWN THE COUNTRY

YOU ARE TOO ILL TO SPEAK YOU MUST GO HOME

NEVER! I SHALL PREACH FOR ONE AND A HALF HOURS INSTEAD.

IN JULY 1916 C.T.STUDD SAILED AGAIN FOR AFRICA WITH EIGHT RECRUITS

HE WAS NEVER TO SEE ENGLAND AGAIN

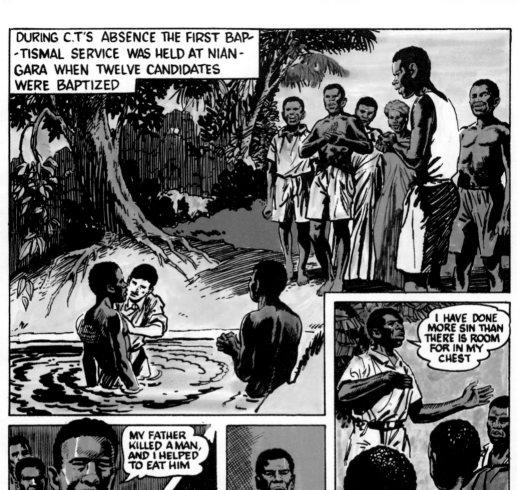

DURING C.T.'S ABSENCE THE FIRST BAP--TISMAL SERVICE WAS HELD AT NIAN-GARA WHEN TWELVE CANDIDATES WERE BAPTIZED

I HAVE DONE MORE SIN THAN THERE IS ROOM FOR IN MY CHEST

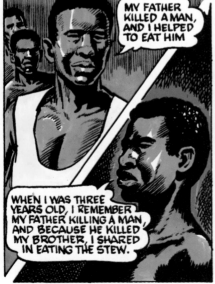

MY FATHER KILLED A MAN, AND I HELPED TO EAT HIM

WHEN I WAS THREE YEARS OLD, I REMEMBER MY FATHER KILLING A MAN AND BECAUSE HE KILLED MY BROTHER, I SHARED IN EATING THE STEW.

I DID WITCHCRAFT WITH THE FINGERNAILS OF DEAD MEN AND WITH THE MEDICINE KILLED A MAN

YET THESE MEN WERE WONDERFULLY CHANGED BY THE POWER OF JESUS, AND BECAME NEW PEOPLE.

39

WHEN C.T. RETURNED TO NALA, HE FOUND GREAT PROGRESS HAD BEEN MADE

HE SETTLED INTO THE WORK AGAIN

ONE DAY:

WE GO NO FURTHER. WE WANT MORE MONEY

GET ON WITH YOUR WORK! REMEMBER IN MY TIME I HAVE EATEN BETTER MEN THAN YOU!

THERE WAS NO MORE TROUBLE AFTER THAT!

A TESTIMONY MEETING

ONE TIME I WAS VERY ILL AND DIED

BUT I ROSE FROM THE GRAVE, AND SAID I HAD SEEN GOD WHO TOLD ME THE ENGLISH WOULD SOON COME AND TELL US THE TRUTH. NOW THEY ARE HERE.

THE FIRST NATIVE PREACHERS WERE SENT OUT—

40

BY THIS AND OTHER MEANS THE WORK CONTINUED TO GROW IN ALL DIRECTIONS.

CHURCHES WERE BUILT

MORE RECRUITS ARRIVED. BY 1923 THERE WERE FORTY MISSIONARIES ON THE FIELD

LATER DISUNITY BEGAN TO APPEAR

C.T. DRIVES US TOO HARD. HE IS A FANATIC

LIVING IN THESE DREADFUL NATIVE HOUSES! WE OUGHT TO BUILD OURSELVES BETTER ONES

CHRISTIANS BECAME LAZY AND WOULD NOT WORK. SOME BACKSLID

O LORD, YOU MUST WORK! GIVE US AN EXPLOSION OF SPIRITUAL DYNAMITE!

WE WILL READ HEBREWS CHAPTER 11 TONIGHT

MOSES

GIDEON

DAVID

DANIEL

"HOW GOD BLESSED THESE MEN AND MADE THEM A BLESSING TO OTHERS CAN IT BE POSSIBLE FOR US TO MARCH UP THE GOLDEN STREET WITH SUCH AS THESE?"

THE HOLY SPIRIT OF GOD CAUSED THESE MEN TO TRIUMPH. HE IS OUR NEED TONIGHT!

ALL WHO ARE WORTHY WILL JOIN THEM, SO THERE'S A CHANCE FOR US YET! GLORY! HALLELUJAH!

WE CAN ILLUSTRATE THIS FROM THE WAR...

"THE SERGEANT-MAJOR WOULD SAY THAT TOMMY COULDN'T CARE LESS WHAT HAPPENS TO HIM SO LONG AS HE DOES HIS DUTY!"

THAT'S WHAT I WANT! LORD, FROM NOW ON I DON'T CARE WHAT HAPPENS TO ME, LIFE OR DEATH, AYE OR HELL, SO LONG AS MY LORD JESUS CHRIST IS GLORIFIED

AMEN!

A NEW BAND WENT OUT THAT NIGHT TO LIVE AND DIE FOR CHRIST

THE WORK WAS NEVER THE SAME AGAIN. CRITICISM DISAPPEARED, LOVE CAME IN, THE BLESSING SPREAD TO THE NATIONAL CHURCH, WHICH WAS REVIVED. THE WORK ADVANCED WITH NEW VIGOUR ON ALL SIDES

42

AT ABOUT 3 a.m. C.T WOULD BE AWAKED BY ONE-LEG, HIS 'BOY'

SOON A CUP OF TEA

ONE-LEG WOULD THEN GO BACK TO SLEEP WHILST C.T. HAD A QUIET TIME WITH GOD.

O LORD, SPEAK TO ME AGAIN FROM YOUR WORD.

DURING THE DAY MANY JOBS HAD TO BE DONE

THAT BEAM IS TOO LONG IT MUST BE SHORTENED

I MUST FINISH THESE LETTERS BEFORE I SET OUT FOR THE PREACHING WEEK-END

TEA CONDENSED-MILK. WHAT ELSE DO I NEED?

IN THE EARLY DAYS HE HAD ALWAYS WALKED, BUT NOW HE WAS TOO WEAK

THE NEWS WOULD SPREAD THAT BWANA HAD ARRIVED AND PEOPE WOULD COME FOR MILES TO THE MEETINGS

IF YOU WANT TO BE SAVED, YOU MUST REPENT, AND BELIEVE, AND FOLLOW JESUS

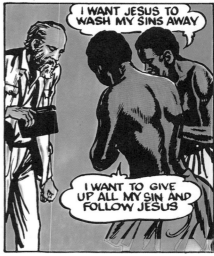

I WANT JESUS TO WASH MY SINS AWAY

I WANT TO GIVE UP ALL MY SIN AND FOLLOW JESUS

C.T. FELT THAT HE COULD NO LONGER LEAVE ALL THE PEOPLE AROUND IBAMBI WITHOUT THE WRITTEN WORD OF GOD — HE STARTED ON THE WORK—

THEY MUST HAVE THE WORD OF GOD. I WILL TRANSLATE THE NEW TESTAMENT INTO KINGWANA.

WHILE HE TRANSLATED JACK HARRISON TYPED

"HE WHO LOSES HIS LIFE FOR MY SAKE WILL FIND IT"

IT'S FINISHED! THE NEW TESTAMENT IN KINGWANA.

GOD'S BOOK IN MY LANGUAGE NOW GOD SPEAKS TO MY HEART.

IN 1928 MRS. STUDD WAS ABLE TO VISIT C.T. FOR TWO WEEKS

WHEN THE TIME CAME FOR HER TO RETURN TO ENGLAND BOTH KNEW THAT THEY WOULD NOT MEET ON EARTH AGAIN

45

IN THE FOLLOWING YEAR HE RECEIVED NEWS OF HER SUDDEN DEATH

SCILLA IS GONE

C.T WAS VERY ILL BY NOW, AND COULD ONLY WORK BY CONSTANTLY TAKING MEDICINE

THE MEETING LASTED FIVE HOURS TO-DAY WONDERFUL!

NEXT DAY —

I FEEL SO ILL AND HAVE SO MUCH PAIN, THE END IS NEAR

A FEW DAYS LATER —

HALLELUJAH! HALLELUJAH!

SO HE PASSED TO HIS REWARD

HIS SCORE IN THE GAME OF LIFE WOULD BE COUNTED, NOT IN HUNDREDS OF RUNS, BUT IN HUNDREDS OF PEOPLE HE HAD WON FOR CHRIST. TODAY, W.E.C. INTERNATIONAL WHICH HE STARTED OPERATES AROUND THE WORLD, WINNING PEOPLE FOR CHRIST IN MANY LANDS.

The End

Many methods used by WEC today were unknown to C.T. Studd, but he would approve of every means that added speed to the evangelisation of the world.

Tools for gospel sharing and Church building have greatly increased during recent years. Those used by WEC include radio, cassettes, printing presses, broadsheets, correspondence courses, agricultural Bible schools and theological education by extension.

Older methods are not neglected. Preaching is primary in all cases, but there is also medical work, translation, literacy programmes and schools. These will always be basic tools for the task, especially in primitive areas.

Representation of WEC at the home end, begun in a simple way by Mrs Studd, has now become a network of activity in Australia, Britain, Canada, Germany, Netherlands, New Zealand, South Africa, Switzerland, USA.

Now a new stage has been reached. Several mission fields are becoming sending bases too, sending men and women to countries beyond their borders. Brazil, France, Hong Kong, and Singapore fall into this category.

SO THE STUDD STORY LIVES ON!

WEC International is an interdenominational and international missionary fellowship serving in more than 40 countries on six continents. It was founded by C.T. Studd in 1913 when he went to what was then the Belgian Congo. His challenging words have become the motto of the mission: "If Jesus Christ be God and died for me, then no sacrifice can be too great for me to make for Him."

Some addresses of WEC International Sending Bases:

Australia:
48 Woodside Avenue, Strathfield, NSW, 2135.

Britain:
Bulstrode, Gerrards Cross, Bucks, SL9 8SZ.

Canada:
37 Aberdeen Avenue, Hamilton, Ontario, L8P 2N6.

New Zealand:
PO Box 27264, Mt Roskill, Auckland 4.

South Africa:
PO Box 47777, Greyville, 4023.

USA:
Box 1707, Fort Washington, Pa 19034.

Missionary Training College:
PO Box 21, St Leonards, Tasmania 7250, Australia.

For a full list of WEC publications write to:
WEC Publications, Bulstrode, Gerrards Cross, Bucks, SL9 8SZ.